TO THE RESCUE!

Rescue at Sea
Around the World

Linda Staniford

capstone

To contact Capstone Global Library please call 800-747-4992, or visit our web site www.capstonepub.com

Edited by Linda Staniford
Designed by Steve Mead
Picture research by Eric Gohl
Production by Victoria Fitzgerald
Originated by Capstone Global Library Ltd
Printed and bound in China

19 18 17 16 15
10 9 8 7 6 5 4 3 2 1

Library of Congress Cataloging-in-Publication Data
Cataloging-in-publication information is on file with the Library of Congress.
Written by Linda Staniford
ISBN 978-1-4846-2753-2 (hardcover)
ISBN 978-1-4846-2757-0 (paperback)
ISBN 978-1-4846-2761-7 (eBook PDF)

Acknowledgments
The author and publisher are grateful to the following for permission to reproduce copyright material:
Alamy: Alan Dawson Photography, 9, David Wingate, 13, Jinny Goodman, 10, Ladi Kirn, 12, 22 (top), Tim Jones, 20, US Marines Photo, 17; DVIC: U.S. Coast Guard/Cutter Healy, back cover (right), 19, 22 (bottom), U.S. Coast Guard/Larry Kellis, 15, U.S. Coast Guard/PO2 Barry Bena, 5, U.S. Coast Guard/PO3 Ross Ruddell, 18; Getty Images: LightRocket/Pacific Press/Ibrahim Khatib, 21; Newscom: Image Broker/Jochen Tack, 6, Photoshot, 11, Photoshot/Angel Manzano, back cover (left), 7, 22 (middle), Photoshot/NHPA/Guy Edwardes, 4, REX/Kazam Media, 14, Stock Connection USA/Craig Lovell, 16, VWPics/Mike Greenslade, 8; U.S. Navy: Air Crewman 2nd Class Darien Durr, cover

Design Elements: Shutterstock

007501RRDS16

Contents

Some words are shown in bold, **like this**.
You can find out what they mean by looking
in the glossary.

Rescue at Sea

The sea can be very **dangerous**. When the wind is blowing hard and the waves are very high, people can quickly get into difficult situations.

A boat's engine can break down, or a member of the crew may need **medical** help. There are different kinds of **emergency** services around the world that can help people who need to be rescued at sea.

Rescue at the Beach

Everyone loves playing on the beach and swimming in the ocean. But swimmers and surfers can quickly be carried out by strong **currents**.

Lifeguards watch out for **emergencies** on busy beaches around the world. They often watch from high up in a tower so that they can see the whole beach.

What Do Lifeguards Do?

Lifeguards keep people safe at the beach. They wear a brightly colored **uniform** so they can be easily seen.

Lifeguards are very good swimmers. If a person is in a difficult situation in the water, a lifeguard can swim out and bring the person back to shore.

How Do Lifeguards Travel?

Lifeguards can go out on the water on a rescue vehicle similar to a jet ski. It can go very fast in **shallow** water.

Lifeguards also have vehicles with big tires. They can drive over very soft sand, close to the water. They can get to people who need help very quickly.

What Happens When There Is an Emergency Out at Sea?

Boats may get into difficult situations out in the water. People on board can use a **marine** radio to call for rescue.

All boats should have **inflatable** life rafts on board. If the boat sinks, the crew can **survive** by floating on these life rafts. They can be easily spotted by rescuers.

How Are People Rescued Out at Sea?

Lifeboats help people who are in difficult situations on boats in the water. There are small, fast, **inflatable** lifeboats for rescuing people close to the shore.

There are also bigger lifeboats that can travel a long way out into the ocean. They can go out in bad storms. They rescue people on boats that have been damaged by the wind and waves.

How Do Aircraft Help Rescue People at Sea?

A helicopter can be used to search for small boats and people in the water. It can pick up injured people and fly them quickly to a hospital.

Seaplanes are sometimes used instead of helicopters to rescue people at sea. They can land on water, but they cannot land if the water is very **rough**.

What If Lifeboats and Planes Can't Get There?

Sometimes people need to be rescued from places that boats or planes can't reach. A helicopter lowers a rescuer into the water. The rescuer swims out to the person and provides **medical** treatment.

In the Antarctic, where it is very cold, ships can become stuck in the ice. A special ice-breaking ship can go through thick ice to reach the **stranded** ship.

Making the World a Safer Place!

Lifeguards and lifeboat crew members are very brave people. They help to make the water safer for us.

It is important to remember the rules for staying safe near the water:

- When you are on the beach, be aware of the tide and any warning signs.
- When you are on a boat, always wear a life jacket.
- Never try to rescue someone yourself. Always call the lifeguard or **emergency** services instead.

Quiz

Question 1
When is a marine radio used?
a) To call for help when a boat is in difficulty
b) When someone needs help on the beach
c) On a jet ski

Question 2
Why does a lifeguard watch from a tower?
a) Because the lifeguard is shorter than other people
b) So the lifeguard can see all of the beach
c) So the lifeguard can dive into the water

Question 3
Where are ice-breaking ships used?
a) On a lifeboat
b) On the beach
c) In the Antarctic

Answers: 1a), 2b), 3c)

Glossary

current movement of water in a river or an ocean

dangerous likely to cause harm or injury

emergency sudden and dangerous situation that must be handled quickly

inflatable can be filled with air

marine relating to the sea

medical relating to helping sick or injured people get better

rough not smooth

shallow not deep

stranded left behind

survive stay alive

uniform special clothes that members of a particular group wear

Find Out More

Books

Chancellor, Deborah. *Sea Rescue* (Emergency Vehicles). Mankato, Minn.: Smart Apple Media, 2014.

Oxlade, Chris. *Rescue at Sea* (Heroic Jobs). Chicago: Raintree, 2012.

Oxlade, Chris. *Rescue Boat* (QEB Emergency Vehicles). Irvine, Calif.: QEB, 2010.

Internet sites

Facthound offers a safe, fun way to find Internet sites related to this book. All of the sites on Facthound have been researched by our staff.

Here's all you do:
Visit www.facthound.com
Type in this code: 9781484627532

Index